# The Green Bean Festival

*"Coloured Bedtime StoryBook"*

*By*

**Nguyen Pham Tu Trinh**

*Illustrated by*

**Linh Chi**

ILLUSTRATED & PUBLISHED
BY
E-KİTAP PROJESİ & CHEAPEST BOOKS

**www.cheapestboooks.com**

 **www.facebook.com/EKitapProjesi**

**ISBN: 978-625-6308-76-3**

Copyright, 2024 by e-Kitap Projesi

Istanbul

**Categories:** Adventure, Community
**Country of Origin:** United States
**Cover:** © Cheapest Books
**License:** CC-BY-4.0

For full terms of use and attribution, http://creativecommons.org/licenses/by/4.0/

Contributing: Linh Chi

**© All rights reserved.**

Except for the conditions stated in the License, no part of this book shall be reproduced or transmitted in any form or by any means, electronic or mechanical, including photocopy, recording or by any information or retrieval system, without written permission form the publisher.

## About the Book

One day, while playing in the green bean fields at her grandmother's house, Nam meets a new friend - a green bean seed. He invites her to meet his family and to join their festival. What new discoveries will she make on her adventure?

This summer, mom sends Mushroom to grandmother's house.

In the morning, Mushroom wakes up early to follow grandma...

To visit the green bean field, the beans are the same length as pencils, smiling at Mushroom playfully.

When the sun goes up high, the grandmother and Mushroom eat green bean rice with sugar together.

It's so cool in the field. And the sound of leaves is so soothing.

"Hello Green bean seed." "Wake up, Mushroom!"

As Mushroom is still surprised, the Green bean already pulls her away.

"I'm green pea."

"I'm bean sprout."

"I'm bean seed."

"I'm a bean seed."

With many stories to tell Tet * is coming. Come with me quickly."

*Vietnamese New Year

Lunar new year

When Grandma puts the beans in the water we turn yellow.

This is banana leaf with pork and sticky rice.

"Banh chung" is square. "Banh tet" is round.

Pickled bean sprouts are added to make the meal good.

Sticky rice in water. Kneaded around small rounded pieces of bean.

Grandma is skillful in wrapping the cakes.

Next to the fermented sticky rice are four-cornered rice dumplings that make the New Year meaningful.

Grandma is arranging the table with sticky cakes and baked cakes.

"Wanna eat?

Wanna eat?" "Mommy piggy and little piggies"

Adding a star-shaped lantern, Mushroom smiles brightly.

Hihihihi...

Grandma smiles, "What are you smiling about?"

Mushroom wakes up, rubbing her eyes.

Grandma asks: "What do you like for dinner?"

"Dessert made with sugar and green bean flour... Rice gruel with green lentils and braised pork...Brussel sprouts with braised fish Beansprouts with tofu."

Mushroom smiles and thinks she will tell grandma the story tonight.

The story is named "The Green Bean Festival".

A poem for Banh chung (square rice dumpling) and Banh tet (round rice dumpling):

> Wrapped inside the leaves
>
> Are sticky rice and green bean
>
> Pork in the center

Again, rice and bean around

One square, one round

Pickles to be included

Besides the apricot blossom

My tet is coming back

A poem for pyramidal glutinous rice cake:

Sticky rice in the ash water

Delicious green bean with stuffing

Crispy and full without stuffing

Dipping in white sugar

Inside the pyramid

Behind the leaf

Like a golden season

Calling for summer

# End of the Story

www.ingramcontent.com/pod-product-compliance
Lightning Source LLC
LaVergne TN
LVHW070451080526
838202LV00035B/2802